ROAD

TO

SUCCESS

Marilyn L. Redmond

BA, CHT, IBRT

EARTH STAR PUBLICATIONS

ROAD TO SUCCESS

Marilyn L. Redmond

EARTH STAR PUBLICATIONS
Cedaredge, Colorado
First Edition
First Printing January 2017
Second Printing March 2017

ISBN 978-0-944851-48-7

The intent of this book is to offer information of a general nature. In the event you use any of the information in this book for yourself is your constitutional right, but the author and publisher assume no responsibility for your actions.

The examples of people's circumstances in this book are composites based on real conditions that exemplify the points being described. My stories are my own experience.

This book may be quoted in part if source and supply address are given.

Dedication

I dedicate this book to my ex-husband. During our marriage, I experienced devastation as well as good times. His desire for becoming a multimillionaire brought grief and hardship through grandiose plans. Through our life mistakes I found the path out of the wasteland into the light that shines brightly today with love and joy. I had to change. He taught me forgiveness, gratitude, unconditional love, and compassion. Because of the wreckage and mistakes during many years, I finally found that inner peace is real success.

Acknowledgments

The *Road to Success* was inspired by the request for chapters for several anthologies about success. I won the honor of my writing appearing in these wonderful books. Because the information is helpful for everyone, it came to me to make the chapters available in another form. I want to thank Kizzi Nkwocha and Patrick Young for selecting me to be part of their writing team for their inspirational books. If you choose to read the complete books which include my chapters, they are listed below.

The Book of Success, "New Glasses Bring Success" © 2015
http://mithrapublishing.com
Hidden Success, "Beyond the Barriers to Success" © 2015
http://mithrapublishing.com
Walking Your Life, "I Wanted to Live" © 2015
http://mithrapublishing.com
Creating Your Life: Mindfulness and Meditation,
"Love Never Fails" © 2015
http://athenapublishing.com

Table of Contents

Finding Success

By Marilyn Redmond

External forces shaped my life;
emphatically they created strife.
Pushing through responsibilities, others' demands,
obligations, in my reality were commands.

Authority spoke strongly to follow.
Punishment, waited for projects undone,
jobs increased and never ceased
will there be a better tomorrow?

My search secured sobriety
After years of casualty
releasing violent voices
from family, church, and society;

Systematically, muting superficial codes
freed my inner voices,
freeing feelings of internal love
I pursue, enjoy my own roads.

A loving source of universal wisdom
loves me daily along my way.
Eternally my personal spirit
cares for me, as I am.

Exploring a new life seems strange
yet, good. Guidance from my heart is true.
Where it leads I do not know; confident that
God awaits as I enjoy my escapade.

Today, I focus on The Great Reality inside,
acclaim a victory with gratitude, delight
for in my soul's reality thrives.
Only there does success abide. © 2014

Chapter One

New Glasses Bring Success

Defining what success means to you provides a basis for achieving your goal. I saw all the glamour and glitter of celebrities, wealthy people, and leaders of the world. After my ballet performances, when I was a little girl, I believed my success was having my name in lights on a marquee. Over the last thirty-one years, the implications of traditional success have changed for me.

When I was married, my husband's intense focus was to become a millionaire as his best friend from the neighborhood became. His motives came from emotional and financial insecurity, lack of self-esteem, and a strong will. Looking to fill his inner void, he left teaching and established a printing business. He was going to make his fortune and become successful. I continued my teaching job to support the family and worked long hours every weekend, vacation, and holiday in the business. I had two jobs for twenty years.

The economic roller coaster of interest rates and other influences affected our yearly business income. Finally, for health reasons we sold the business, got a divorce and went our separate ways. We divided our remaining assets, equally. His desire to be a millionaire took him to Palm Springs, California, to buy commercial property during a low market. Ultimately, he became bankrupt after more economic dives.

Fortunately, my desire to be a millionaire was not my highest ambition. Because of illness, I medically retired from teaching. I needed to find a healthy lifestyle. My new focus was to change my mind-set to a rational, contributing, selfless member of society as an individual. Rather than selfish motives for success, I found it very rewarding to share and contribute to others. This manifests in feelings of success. Today, I know success comes from the inside and projects out.

Investing in new training and classes brought a new twist to my teaching path into counseling/hypnotherapy, writing, speaking, and teaching adults. Over a little by little progression, life began to flower. In addition, my financial investments increased steadily. With this new affluence, I paid off all my debts. I kept doing the next indicated project that was there for me. Most importantly, I learned to listen to my inner guidance.

Instead of pursuing fame and fortune, I attracted the right people, and opportunities to me for a change in a new way of life. Life comes together in wonderful ways as I allow it to happen. Accomplishing the foundation upon which to build comes first. Slowly my new motivation created a constructive basis. I altered my goal for a higher realistic consciousness, rather than an iconic status that is fleeting. Ultimately, it produced excellent results.

I have several different hats and talents that I take pleasure in, and one or another seemed to become a focus alternately. My career was continuing to attract clients and opportunities with time off for vacations. However, I was concerned that my income would not be as big as my wishes and dreams. Learning money management skills and discipline paid off. Interestingly, I could cover my expenses and my needs were met.

Gradually, I began to feel better about my life and myself. Over the years, I realized that I had created financial security while enjoying my work. I found work less difficult and more fun. Through my singular motivation to change my life from past trauma and crisis, with a daily focus my career has moved forward steadily. In addition, I have become fiscally secure.

One Saturday morning I was driving to Seattle to present a program. My silent voice said, "You are a success." I realized that my inner success meant more than my name in lights, a large bank account, or a huge following of hanger-on's. It was an inside job and the outward circumstances arrive from my inner mind-set of helping others, being sincere, and caring. I felt terrific.

What Prevented Success Sooner?

Recycling repeatedly old ideas, and then expecting different results, needed to change. I found that the classes and support groups I found were perfect for me. I needed new information. I wanted new healthy ways to go forward.

Not realizing how much my family background of alcoholism and mental illness had been the modeling for my life, I needed to change those inner messages, beliefs, and behaviors. Learning that my life was based in fear and from negative emotions was a revelation. It was time to address my fear, anger, and resentments. My other emotions as guilt and shame needed to go, too. My family's beliefs were limiting me. All this negativity were messages prompted from the ego. I was surviving in an ego-based life of fear, which had attracted a domestic violent marriage.

All of the above emotions and attitudes stopped my dreams that I tried so hard to achieve. I always felt lonely, not good enough, and financially insecure. My mother was an expert in guilt. When I did have achievements, my shame stopped me from enjoying them. Shame came from childhood abuse and magnified through church teachings. I was a good victim. If I dressed nicely, then I was acceptable.

Seeing that society looks for what is wrong and not what is right, showed me new understanding. Medicine looks for the medical problems and they seem to get worse or new ones come along. My church told me what was wrong with me and I was not good enough. Schools have changed into more testing to label students failures if they do not meet certain left-brain standards. In addition, the justice system is about what is wrong and punishment. These messages dwell on limiting my abilities, health, education, and spiritual growth.

As a teacher, I always had excellent evaluations and knew I was a good teacher. I left my teaching position that was my only sense of security. I medically retired for several health reasons. My life up to then had exhausted me and I was not healthy enough to continue in an 8 to 5 position. However, everything in my life was falling apart. I knew I was smart because I was valedictorian in high school and had seven years of college. Why was my world a failure?

How to Overcome Your Obstacles

Denial is the number one offender. I was honest paying for my groceries, but I was not honest with myself. In my dysfunctional family, it was not possible to have reality or honesty. I continued this deception until I had to make a decision about my existence. During a life and death crisis, I declared that I wanted to live and not die. This choice brought honesty into my life. I had to become as honest as I could if I were to become sane and healthy.

I had to move out of my head and into my heart. That meant I needed to walk in faith and not live from my ego. Instead of setting up all the ducks to shoot in a row, like the concession at the circus, I needed to allow the universe to bring me the right results. I needed to trust the universe. I could no longer run my life from fear. Moving into trusting a loving universe to support me in my life was a major decision.

This was a big step for me. I always tried to arrange the checkerboard and knew my jumps ahead of time. Without my predicting the results, I was uncertain to the outcome. At one point, it became obvious to me that I had to let the chips fall where they would, I had no control over what happened. Surprisingly to me, the energy felt good and it fell together better than I expected. In fact, it went together pretty well; however, the feelings were limited, because I had only partial faith.

I became aware that if I chose 100% faith, I could get even better results and feel terrific. The more I opened up to this invisible, beneficent energy, the better my life became. I chose to become open-minded to all the good outcomes. I had been the one stopping my success. Learning a spiritual axiom that what I focus on grows brought a new focus; I needed my main emphasis to be on truth.

Tools to Triumph

With pen and paper, I began to take an inventory of all my fears, anger/resentments and behaviors I had learned growing up, that were preventing a better life. I listed each one with complete honesty. In each case in the past, I had blamed others for my problems; I found this gave my power to them. This left me feeling powerless and hopeless. I realized that all the time it was of my own doing. I was a good victim. I had been hurting myself, while they did not even know how desperate I was.

I had pointed my finger at those people being my problems, while three fingers pointed back at me. It did not take long to recognize that I was the enemy and I had to take responsibility for myself and how I conducted my life. Taking responsibility for my life included making amends to those I harmed in the past. Owning up to my selfishness, dishonesty, and self-centeredness was not easy. However, it became necessary to be honest in all parts of my life. It actually freed me. I could move from volunteering to be a victim into being the victor.

Therapeutic Hypnosis and meditation addresses the root cause of my pain and suffering that is blocking my true inheritance. Trauma, abuse, or violence can be hidden until later years of life. Hypnosis is a simple way to release the resistance in life's struggles into a new higher consciousness of understanding. Regression therapy offers the opportunity to heal those things from childhood that are repressed and became survival mechanisms. However, when you become an adult, it becomes time to resolve these issues and move forward into an emotionally mature place.

As I released each negative thought, communication, or conduct and replaced it with love and grace, I grew into a new person. This filled my inner void with the truth of who I am. I was not dependent on what my family or society said about me any longer. I could stop reacting to situations around me and begin to respond in loving responses to others and myself.

An inventory identifies my past and worries about the future, which is where my head had been for all this time. Even though I looked like an adult, my scared little girl was there. I was not getting my way and life was not the way I wanted. I saw my immaturity in reacting with anger. My fears dissolved in faith. Moreover, I do not have to guilt myself. The regressions released painful emotions and then restored a new picture into a loving healed solution.

Raising my consciousness into being in the present left the past fearful influences behind. One day, clarity came and I saw that life was not good or bad, only that my emotional reaction was based in the past responding from my history. There is nothing to fear if I walk in faith. *Right now I am safe, I have what I need, and my needs are met.* My energy shifts from the past drama into a confidence and trust in the universal support that is beneficent. I understand that each experience is a lesson for me to respond in love. It was time to see life as it is — life is — instead of how I wanted it to be.

Learning about universal laws made this easier. Obeying the speed limit when driving is necessary or the consequence is a speeding ticket. However, there are other laws that control our lives that are not written down. These laws are the blueprint for our lives to work that are invisible. When I apply them, the consequences are fruitful. The consequence for not aligning with them will ultimately bring me to a place of surrender.

It was time to move into the "NOW." This is where I can find the courage, answers, and opportunities. Being in the *present* is a gift of personal power, when it is used rightly. I had to align my energy with the universal love that was in my heart. The right use of will power is the secret.

Universal Laws Affect Your Life

As a child, I was treated like a Shirley Temple doll, so I had no feelings. In addition, I was taught to be seen and not heard.

Therefore, my energy did not move. All my fears stopped my progressing into maturity. I found that people are energy fields and energy moves and vibrates at different levels. I had been stuck most my life in the lower vibrations of fear and had no tools to change that. This changes when you observe the Universal Laws and release all negative emotions and behaviors. Real communications and sharing feelings move energy into higher vibrations of love.

Albert Einstein understood this when he said, "No problems can be solved from the same level of consciousness that created it." Universal laws are based in the Law of Love. Changing my thoughts, words, and actions so they function in the universal plan of love made the difference. At this level, my development is not stopped and my progress can evolve. I can outgrow the past. Now, I am sending out positive energy to others and feel good about myself.

There are many Universal Laws; however, there are four that can alter your life, quickly. The first law to examine is The Law of Cause and Effect. It says that I reap what I sow. If I send self-centered emotions to get what I want, the effect will not be productive at some point. Being selfish is negative energy and has no power. I caused my own problems. When my motivation changed to giving instead of receiving, my life improved. Do you choose loving experiences to return? It will come back. A popular saying is "What goes around comes around."

I thought I was a loving mother and wife. Nevertheless, in reality I was defending myself to be safe from childhood abuse I had endured. That is what came back to me. I had to become defenseless. Therefore, I learned fairly quickly to send loving ideas, well being, prosperity, abundance and/or health to others. It smoothes the path and returns with wonderful feelings. My estranged relationships have mended from continuing this. I believe this has also brought my feelings of financial security, abundance, and self-esteem.

The next law is the "Law of Attraction." My intuition told me I had to become what I wanted. I will attract what I am, when I move into a mind-set and vibration of my desire. This lesson was a big one. I had been in a disastrous marriage and wanted a loving relationship. In the movie *The Secret*, they forgot to tell people to change yourself to be what you want to attract.

I made a list of the five most important things I desired in a new partner. I released old ideas, beliefs, and fears. Over time, I was changing. Instead of looking for tall, dark, and handsome in a husband, I found I was more interested in the character of the person. Spirituality, honesty, loyalty, and sincerity became my focus. I gradually began developing into a new person through lots of work and time. I attended a spiritual study group and found a man who I knew had the inner qualities that attracted my attention. We have been together in a relationship of uncon-ditional love for 15 years. I am in a successful relationship.

This law also works for abundance and prosperity. My parents lived through the Great Depression and the family mantra was, "We can't afford that." Driving home one day on the freeway, I felt an inner feeling of intense abundance and prosperity. It moved to surround me in the car. That feeling extended from the car to the highway, then past the highway to the shoulders and further. The energy felt like it extended beyond my vision. I felt I was swallowed up in an energy that provided everything I needed.

Abundance and Prosperity was there for me and I was in it. There were no limits to its existence. This secured my feelings of financial success. Everything was there for me; I knew my needs were taken care of. Successfully, I had changed the energy from my childhood that had been a huge issue.

Nowadays, I attract the right clients that match my expertise. They often appear from word of mouth, the internet, and unknown circumstances. If I have a presence in like-minded organizations, show up at events, and have an internet presence, they find me. I recently had to turn away a client as my plate was full.

The next law is "Like Attracts Like." This law can bring disastrous or great results. My Cinderella-like growing up attracted people to my life with similar dysfunctional back-grounds. My teaching also attracted dysfunctional classrooms of students. In my printing business, often employees with similar problems as my husband and myself were hired, which was not good for the business. This additional drama and crisis of the help distracted from doing business. The good employees left because conditions were not harmonious and healthy.

Today, my life is pleasant, busy, and the workflow is usually smooth. It has been a challenge to pace myself from being a workaholic to a normal pace. In addition, it is a huge shift to allow the universe to decide the best for me. However, the necessary elements come together with surprises as I go with the flow, instead of pushing through to make it happen. Not every-thing goes like I want, but it works out in the overall. The results tend to be better than I expect.

It took a long time to find the right publisher for my past books. Then my publisher said that she would not be able to continue because of sickness. I allowed things to fall in place; I started looking for another publisher. I was not in a hurry because I was ill at the time, myself. This publisher was wonder-ful to work with and I did not really want to start another search. Her expertise and talents fit my publishing needs well. A short time later, before I was ready to move forward, she contacted me. She would again be available. The universe brought her back as my publisher. I know we fit together well.

Another universal law is "The Law of Giving and Gratitude." The energy has to flow. It begins by giving, which opens available space for it to return in appropriate forms back to fill that open space. Getting in that flow allows the increase, because the energy expands when released. This brings abundance. When receiving my prosperity, I then offer gratitude and thankfulness for this ample reward and return of success.

When I receive with appreciation, it allows more to come my way. I write "Thank you, God" on my bank deposits. This demonstrates that I am open to receiving and continuing to share with others. Over time, this becomes more prosperity and success. Some people say you have to *give it away to keep it.*

Growing up, I was taught to hang on to every penny out of desperation. I believe that becoming more generous in my giving to charity, friends in need, and financially helping family when necessary has brought a new level of happiness and prosperity into my life. When I change this attitude to sharing appropriately to causes that are important to me, I find a new avenue of my life lifting into a better place. It feels good to contribute. I see it today as giving to myself, because in spirit we are all one.

Acceptance of Reality

Your escrow of success is waiting for access through your experience. The past dilemmas and mind-set stop the flow of energy moving into new places to manifest. In addition, past emotional and religious beliefs stopped this flow. Moreover, hanging on to worries blocked the stream. They prevented being available and present. When releasing these barriers, reality can happen. I no longer need to see the bad more than the good. It is all good!

As a "doer" and controller, I liked to make sure everything was in order, organized, ready to go. When I am "being" in the present, the obstacles leave, allowing the energy to flow to me. These gifts of abundance, prosperity and success have been there all the time. Now, I am open to receiving them as they appear in my life. I thank the universe for the gifts. This allows more to come. The fearful veil is lifted to see beyond to what was waiting for me. It was waiting beyond the fear to improve and enhance my life.

Accepting this brings growth in my comfort zone. The anxiety of growing into a new consciousness is only temporary until the feelings of reality become more common. I gave up all my beliefs, because, I "know" everything that is right for me will manifest at the right time and in the correct way. Allowing the loving benefits of the universe into my life is a new experience; it can be an adventure. It works.

When you replace the negativity with loving energy, your confidence, self-acceptance, and security is assured. It never left you; you were not aligned with it. You were never "not a success" as society tries to convince us. There is nothing wrong with you and there never has been.

The blinders and earplugs of the past fearful visions and skewed messages are gone. There is a song, "On a Clear Day You Can See Forever." This creates an elevated awareness. The clouds of fear lift and the sunlight is brilliant. Denial, resistance, and struggles leave with *joyous acceptance* for your new understanding, knowing, and happenings.

In new receptivity, it happens. You can now accept yourself as a successful person and see others as the caring people they are. The universal laws will flow easily, bringing help and good fortune. Opportunities and clients will appear at the ideal time and in the proper situations. You know and trust that the universe is taking care of you. You are a success!

A New Pair of Glasses

Having cleaned off the lenses of your glasses from the debris of the past and future, you now see that *life is.* Now you see that it started with you. You brought on the hardships from your old ideas and beliefs. Life did not do it to you. You become empowered. Instead of reacting from fear, it is easy to see that life is neutral and it was your own emotions that made it seem good or bad based in your past and future history. Life is not good or bad, *life is.* You move forward in confidence. It is the path to grow into seeing yourself from the truth of who you are.

Life has the necessary lessons and tests to help you advance into a higher view and a bigger picture of who you are. Life around you is flawless. It is exactly as it needs to be. It is your choice how to react or respond to the events that face you. When you choose to take action consistently in love, life blooms.

Each event along the way moved me closer to being genuine. The tests along the way are just another opportunity to prove that I can accept what life brings to me joyously. This maturity is long sought by many. Now you can choose to create a new reality of success.

Shakespeare was right.

"All the world's a stage,
And all the men and women merely players;
They have their exits and their entrances,
And one man in his time plays many parts."

The people around you played their parts for you to find yourself and change into the success that you always have been. In forgiving those who were causing difficulty for you, you release the bondage of the emotional ties to that person or situation. You realize they were actually helping you. Your attitude will change and realize that they were acting out a fault in yourself for you to identify for your healing. When you are able to thank them in your prayers for bringing it to your attention, more wholeness will occur.

Helping others to find their success is an important part, too. You will benefit more than those you are assisting from new understanding, wisdom, and sharing your hard-knock story. With new players coming into your world to reflect your new-found success, the only aspiration is up.

Life is the art of allowing. Allow all the good things to come to you that are in your escrow from the universe. Learning not to fight, resist or sabotage your success is another lesson. Acceptance of life's lessons is not easy, but resolves the barriers to success.

Many parts of your past fade in the sunlight. No longer are you forcing results for gain. At this point not consenting to let people, events, or opportunities happen, as they will, puts a monkey wrench in your success. It comes at the right time, with the right results that will produce better outcomes than your plans. Life is in perfect order, when you cooperate.

Business owners appear on a program called "Shark Tank." They are looking for financing and expertise to grow their venture. Sometimes several contestants on the television program did not get the business funding they were seeking. This show has wealthy financiers who pick participants that they feel have a solid basis with which to collaborate. The five investors are called the "sharks."

In this show, several times, I did not think the person would receive the money requested for various reasons. Surprisingly, when the whole stories of their struggles were told, one of the panel members usually would step up to the plate. Each shark related to the difficulties, such as a family refinancing a home to produce the necessary business funds, a family home becoming the location for a fledging factory, or living in a car as all the money was being put into the future of the business and they were homeless. The contestants were being themselves.

Those contenders that missed the support of a shark found success, too. They were glad they were not picked as their success took a different but better path. Opportunities came to them from their appearance on the program. Later these entrepreneurs were glad that they did not hook up with a shark because their new prospects were better and fit them well for bigger successes. Alternate prospects grew beyond their entrepreneurs' dreams.

Cooperating with life brings the life for which you were searching and desiring. Your new role brings empowerment, faith, and balance. Trusting the universe through this process brings the prosperity, abundance, and happiness desired. With your new glasses, you see that it is all good. You are a success. You attract success!

Chapter Two

Beyond the Barriers to Success

"If we were talking to you on your first day here, we would say, 'Welcome to planet Earth. There is nothing that you cannot be or do or have. And your work here – your lifetime career – is to seek joy.'" ~ Abraham

Do you feel like the joyful success in your life is missing? Is it hidden from your perception and experience? Now is the time to reveal this missing element. Society has conditioned fears into all parts of our lives along with terms that stop our awareness of true triumph. Selfish has become the new meaning for self-care. Addiction was replaced with a new definition, abusing a substance. These all bring a new understanding to a word that originally told truth. Failure has become a word that produces shame.

Over time the meaning of many words are distorted and used against us. Is there really failure? This comment comes from judging another to make the speaker look good in comparison. Alternatively, it can make the other person feel less and unworthy. Telling someone that they are not successful has become a way to reduce self-esteem, especially in the school system.

Thomas Alva Edison, who was an American inventor and business person, said that he was not a failure. He developed many devices that greatly influenced life around the world, including the phonograph, the motion picture camera, and a long-lasting, practical electric light bulb. "I haven't failed. I've just found 10,000 ways that don't work," he commented about his many attempts to invent the electric light bulb.

He seemed to be quite wise in life. He remarked, "Many of life's failures are people who did not realize how close they were to success when they gave up." Another of his comments is, "When you have exhausted all possibilities remember this: you haven't." Another observation by him about accomplishment is, "Opportunity is missed by most people, because it is dressed in overalls and looks like work."

What kind of work relates to success? Why does it delude you? This is the rest of the story.

There are two kinds of success. What others think of you in society can bring high acclaim, money and honors. Does it pump up your ego so you look good to others? Do you like the attention and acclaim? Is the limelight lifelong or your 15 minutes of fame, fleeting? Is social success brief or sustainable? Alternatively, does inner success bring eternal, lasting, and contentment that we call joy? Do you believe doing the right thing is never wrong no matter what others think? Is being comfortable in your own skin important? Is your self-esteem enough to validate yourself? Which explanation of success is yours?

I wanted validation, acceptance, and peace in my life, because my life was chaotic and dysfunctional from childhood and my marriage. I accomplished success as valedictorian from high school. I soloed with a symphony on the flute. In addition to being the first in my family to graduate from college, I received the honor of *cum laude*. I always had high evaluations on my teaching ability over the many years I taught school. I looked like a success in my job, family, and community. However, I felt unwanted, lacked self worth, and peace of mind.

I ultimately realized that personal fulfillment for success required me to apply new tools to my endeavor. My new tools became honesty, open-mindedness, and willingness. These opened the door to a new life where I could find inward achievement.

I always paid my bills and never thought of myself as not being honest. I looked good to others; however, I lacked self-honesty. I had a clean house, taught school, belonged to the right organizations, took my children to their activities and never complained. Nevertheless, I was dying from poor medical protocol and my fearful state of mind. My insides and my outsides did not match. It was time to say, "I want a happy life and to feel good inside."

Becoming open-minded was another big challenge for me. My family was not open-minded. Growing up, I learned it was my stepfather's way or the highway. We looked good in church, but I was told what happens at home stays at home and what happens at church stays at church. The physical, mental, emotional, and spiritual abuse I endured was not discussed or ever addressed. Thirty years after I graduated from college, he mused, "We never got you a graduation gift, did we?" There were no opinions but his. He was the "God" of the family. I needed to be open-minded to a loving Heavenly Father, a Creator that would accept me the way I was.

The tricky one for me was willingness. I did not know how to begin with this one. However, I was told, "be willing, to be willing." That seemed to do the trick. Gradually, I found that Shakespeare was right, "The readiness is all." I was eager to give up my miserable life for a better one. I understand today that life is about choice and free will. I could choose to align with a loving universal energy within and have better results.

I realized that fear in my life had stopped many successes. I became willing to release all the barriers to the love that was in my heart. Realizing and identifying that guilt, shame, anger, jealousy, and other negative feelings are forms of fear was a new understanding to me. They were obstacles to my achieving beyond my fear-based life. I discovered and released what was obscuring my accomplishments and achievements. I had been my worst enemy.

I became willing to let love be my guide. I preferred love to be my new motivation. Love is a choice. Over time, I came up with a new purpose. *What is the most loving action for you and for me?* This changed my consciousness from reacting as a victim bemoaning "poor me," into responding with considerate and thoughtful behaviors.

Because I was not acknowledged in my family for my achievements or worthiness, I did not give myself the honor I deserved. I was not only missing the acknowledgement from my parents, but I discounted and minimized my own successes. I did not see what I had achieved as worthwhile because I did not feel worthwhile.

I saw a movie called *A Beautiful Mind* in 2001. It is an American biographical drama film based on the life of John Nash, a Nobel Laureate in Economics. He was diagnosed with mental illness. At the end of the film, his life seemed normal. When asked what happened, he replied, "I gave up listening to the voices in my head." It was also time for me to change my voices in my mind to praise myself for actions and undertakings that were productive, helpful, and contributed to others. As I found my own self-esteem and became worthy, I was able to see my contributions and activities as genuine successes. I had stopped my own successful feelings.

Edison was right, it does take work. For over thirty years, I have searched daily to identify and apply new life skills. These replace the old fearful ideas, behaviors and thoughts that were unconstructive. This has created a new foundation upon which to build my inner thriving mind-set. Through this search, I became fearless. It is an inside job.

Socrates said, "The unexamined life is not worth living." Over many years of self-searching, I found that my thinking was obscuring my inner truth of success with childish and selfish reactions from old disturbances. My motivations were self-seeking and my life was lacking love.

My success was buried deep inside under the painful trauma and drama of my growing up and destructive marriage. Surprisingly, today my outer successes are manifesting from my new inner understanding and knowledge that has brought balance and harmony to my life. I feel successful today.

Currently, my experiences are producing successful opportunities for which I did not plan or search. I am attracting new happy projects and activities that seem almost effortless at times. My heart became open to being a conduit of help and love to others.

Finally, realizing that the family's rage was projected onto me and I was carrying their anger was a huge awakening. I shouldered their lack of success, too. Forgiveness releases us from the painful past. The people, places and events around you reflect the very parts of you that need mercy and love, so you can return to wholeness and joy.

Dr. Gerald Jampolsky states, "Forgiveness is letting go of all hopes for a better past." Your friends and enemies play a very important role for you, which you requested before this lifetime. You plan the events with your masters and guides before you incarnate. Accepting the circumstances you requested for your growth is important to releasing the emotional attachments. Sending love, gratitude, forgiveness, and compassion is the lesson that changes the energy you came to transform. Your loving response in each life incident restores your soul.

Do not be put off by the uncomfortable emotions that arise as you do this work, for it is merely the release of painful memories from the past now surfaced. You buried them deep in the subconscious parts of your mind. To do so was necessary to avoid going into deep depression or even despair when you were younger; however, they did expand and smolder within your memory. Now they can be released in their surfacing to leave. In healing, you see how you allowed them to inflate and grow over time.

The bridge between the duality in the material world and the oneness of a higher consciousness of love is forgiveness. I recently heard at a lecture a discussion about what is forgivable. The answer is—It is all forgivable. In spirit, there are no actions that are too bad not to forgive. When I thanked those people in my meditations that caused me the most anguish in the past, my energy changed. Immediately, I felt no influence from those old terrible times. I felt current and in the present moment.

In reality, all is viewed as equal in value, because otherwise is to see judgment. Therefore, all miracles are also equal without one being bigger than another is. *It is, what it is,* has become a familiar saying. "As forgiveness allows love to return to my awareness, I will see a world of peace and safety and joy." *A Course in Miracles*, W 89

It is important to forgive yourself for putting yourself through such horrible criticism and condemnations from others as real. In *A Course in Miracles*, it states, "God gave the Holy

27

Spirit to you, and gave Him the mission to remove all doubt and every trace of guilt that His dear Son has laid upon himself. It is impossible that this mission fail." T 82

Releasing the judgment of yourself and others allows space for learning love, faith, and trust. Understand that your thinking created the emotional reactions from fear. They were all based in illusion. When you realize that only what God creates is Real, and your thinking is an illusion, it is easy to release the old emotional ties. They dissipate into the ethers.

Your new understanding from this elevated realization and application brings feelings of caring and compassion. Without them, you would not be the new person today that you are. "No one is where he is by accident and chance plays no part in God's plan." *A Course in Miracles*, M 25

You are in the audience as the curtain now falls on the end of your play. Pretend others are on a stage in front of you. You stand and applaud vigorously. Bravo! They played their parts so well that you believed it completely. The illusion is over. You now see beyond the performance into spirit. You can see the love in their hearts beyond the parts they played for you to change. It becomes time to empower yourself instead of staying the victim.

With further understanding, I found that I had created the lessons for my maturity and to heal my karma. Those people and circumstances played out the parts I requested to show me how to grow and heal. I thanked them in my vision and realized I had made it up. It was like an illusion or dream and I can wake up. What my mind makes up is not real.

This new understanding brought a deeper insight to what was hidden in my life. My "inner light" was blocked by all the fear of societal conditioning with judgments, criticisms, and condemnations. I was looking at appearances and not beyond.

Success is opening the doors to my heart so that the inner light can manifest out as love, success, abundance, and peace. The fears were like clouds blocking my heritage and birthright.

Courage to open the door to my heart is to embrace life and all its beauty. To embrace joyfully all parts of the wonderful and incredible me! I was always a success in the eyes of my Creator.

The release of these emotional memories offers unconditional love to those who caused them and to you, as well. This will bring you a welcome sense of peace as you start to feel the uplifting energies nudging you towards a feeling of success.

Love heals all karma. Love glues your shattered soul's pieces back into its whole. With this shift into a compassionate completely open heart, you return to God-consciousness. You now see through the eyes of God, the eyes of love. It is all love. You see the good in everything!

My favorite song is *The Impossible Dream.* As Don Quixote says, "The mission of each true knight ... his duty-nay, his privilege!" He sings about wanting to overcome the negative messages in his mind that obscured his success. This is not about agreeing with it, necessarily, but understanding how you summoned it and why it may have stung. Because, yeah, you did attract it, and it does not have to sting anymore. You take responsibility for your whole life.

A daily saying sent out from "The Universe" on the internet stated, "The beginner scorns criticism. The wise soul carefully weighs it. And the Master says, 'But, of course!'"

Your Focus Changes

Joy becomes your consciousness, as fear no longer exists. Some people call this being reborn. "To be born again is to let the past go, and look without condemnation upon the present" is another quote from *A Course in Miracles* T 234. You are born again into a completely loving spirit that fills your inner life. You become unafraid. You are a channel of love and peace. You are a love giver instead of a love seeker.

Moving into living in the "Now" is the *presence of God's grace* called the Fifth Dimension. Healing your broken soul through love returns you to being a "Whole Spirit"; you truly are a *holy spirit*. We are all one in spirit, a beneficial energy that fills and surrounds all of us. All there is, is love.

No longer do the past harms and fears or future worries direct your life; you are free from old emotional baggage by this point. You no longer have opinions, judgments or beliefs. You have a new freedom letting go of egocentric, selfish, and self-centered earlier motives. Happiness fills the void left by undoing the ego's power. **Love is left when releasing everything unloving**. Self-esteem is restored and successfully emotional security returns.

Your inward feelings become fulfillment, triumphant, and contentment. You have a sense of prosperity, abundance, and safety that all is well. Having enough, being satisfied, and feeling rich in spirit flowers. Loving emotions of stillness and serenity replace your inner emptiness. A smile comes to your face as you enjoy your newfound success of inner peace. Because your needs are met, you are able to see where you can be helpful to others.

This quantum leap moves you beyond the old paradigm of linear time. You do not see the other person as separate and to blame, but one with you in spirit. Releasing the emotional connections of resentment, guilt, or revenge allows the realization that your brain created your false impressions; they were not real. This person agreed to help you with your lessons.

Thanking them rather than separating from them as if they are the bad person, brings unity of spirit.

Quantum physics is about unity, so is the Fifth Dimension and beyond. You have grown past your old consciousness of separation. Your old reactions are not your first response anymore. *How can you lend a hand* in your new forward action?

Revealing Love, the Real Success

Society, medicine, and religions teach you to look without for your answers instead of seeing what is within, the real you. Rarely do you find someone who is yearning for immortality who shuts his or her eyes to what is without and behold the inner Self. Yet, when the outer distractions and beliefs leave, knowing arrives and success is found. Your beneficent inner power called spirit is experienced. You see beyond appearances, the invisible becomes clear.

"Sometimes you walk into things, that, if you were paying attention, vibrationally, you would know right from the beginning that it wasn't what you are wanting. In most cases, your initial knee-jerk response was a pretty good indicator of how it was going to turn out later. The things that give most of you the most grief are those things that initially you had a feeling response about, but then you talked yourself out of it for one reason or another."

~ Abraham

Love is the highest power in creation and underlying harmony of the Universe. It is the supreme law whereby you throw off the bonds of separateness and perceive the great spiritual unity in which we have our fundamental essence. Happiness is a function of releasing your wants and desires for "Thy Will Be Done." Accepting the love within produces happiness.

You become a channel of love, the highest vibration. It moves into the highest realization labeled unconditional love, light, or God. You are successfully channeling love to yourself and those around you.

Letting go of self-defeating ways allows the spirit to grow in gentleness and clarity. Through love, you serve; which brings prosperity, abundance, and well-being, which is real success. These could be called the fruits of the spirit mentioned in Galatians 5:22-23 of the Bible. "But the fruit of the Spirit is love, joy, peace, longsuffering, gentleness, goodness, faith, meekness, temperance: against such there is no law." The spiritual connection between you and others becomes evident. You are effectively bearing the fruit of the spirit, which is love.

Attracting Success through Higher Vibrations

When studying Edgar Cayce, I first heard the principle, "Everything is vibratory." It made sense to me in understanding God as spirit. Everything is a vibrating energy in different planes, including your thinking about illness, scarcity, and even relationships. Higher vibrating energy is in good health, abundance and loving relationships. The vibrations range from the very negative, fearful ways of thinking to the highest and truest. When you journey through all degrees, you reveal yourself and find God. "For without passing through each and every stage of development, there is not the correct vibration to become one with the creator." Edgar Cayce

To improve your environment, focus upon the best things currently around you until you flood your own vibrational patterns with thoughts of appreciation. Finally, start a gratitude list that you add to daily to keep your focus on thankfulness. You need to lift all self-imposed limitations—all limitations are self-imposed—and free yourself to receive wonderful things. With changed vibrations, you can then allow the new-and-improved conditions and circumstances to come into your experience.

Ask yourself, "What do I want?" Take one of your wants and ask yourself the following questions: How will I change when I get this want? How will my life change when I get this? What do I see my life looking like when I get this want?

In the moment, with your new state of being vibrating your own unique vibration, with no agendas or planning, you create your new life by attracting like energies in perfect synchronicity and timing. No one can deny you or grant you anything. You attract your success by matching the vibration.

My inner self can release the blockages and obstacles in meditation along with other supportive help. In addition, applying alternative health methods raise my vibrations. A few hints to help raise vibrations are flower essences, acupuncture, and tuning forks. These break the blocks that are stopping the energy from flowing and rising for the ability to move into a higher dimensional mind-set. I move past my fears of the lower vibrations. By facing my fears, I became fearless. What a feeling! "For he, or she, that is without fear is free indeed." — Edgar Cayce

A New Approach Brings Success

A few years ago, I had to replace my skylight. The contractor put in another style that was not attractive. He did not discuss this with me before he picked a different style. I was upset as it spoiled the view of the woods, clouds, and sky when looking out. I asked for it to be corrected with the same design of my original one. His bullying and lies were complicating the disagreement. In the past, I would have submitted to his controlling anger that resulted. I found it hard to stand up for myself in the past, especially to harassment.

I found out that it was possible to obtain the same model as my old one. Moreover, that there was no law that prohibited my having it. In addition, I filed a complaint with a business bureau where he had a high rating. Ultimately, he put in the acceptable skylight. I had successfully stood up for what was right. Through staying in the facts of the situation, I was able to triumph in this dispute of his trying to manipulate a situation that was not acceptable to me. My not backing down was a huge success for me.

This occurrence was the opportunity for me to move beyond my past into a better path of standing up for myself. Successfully I came from strength instead of the old victim I had been for years. I found myself to be the pot of gold at the end of the rainbow. I was the genie in the lamp of Aladdin.

Recently, when I became fearless, I found a new understanding about myself. There was nothing wrong with me. I was never a mistake. My life was not in error. It is important to accept that everything in life is as if it is supposed to be. This brought real awareness into my life.

People are right where they are in their journey. Situations actually brought new perspectives to my life even when at the time they seemed overwhelming and devastating. New insights brought new clarity and victory to my life.

I have found a simple way for the genie inside to find the reality that is buried deep down inside of my soul. It is in applying three principles. The first one is knowing that the only power is God. *You shall have no other gods before me;* this means to keep your focus always on God, any other focus becomes a false god.

The second is to neutralize the emotions surrounding the person or event that is the focus. It is not harmful, hurtful, or destructive, but a "lesson" for you to identify the energy which needs to shift into love, compassion, forgiveness, and gratitude.

It becomes your lesson and mirror. The person's face could be anyone and the circumstances could be different; however, it is your energy reflecting back to you for change.

Lastly, there is no good and evil, the devil, or any other power, because God did not create them. You made it up. You made them up in your mind. What God creates is Reality. What you create is nothingness.

The key to staying in reality is consistently to remind yourself throughout the day and night that you are in this special place. **I am in joy, in gratitude and in the presence of God.** This is Reality. This mind-set creates grace. God's grace is sufficient. Enjoy this serenity and peace of mind wherever you are. You always have been a success. You will attract successes.

How Do I Experience My Hidden Happiness?

Maybe you have felt that love has eluded you. It was buried under the fearful past and unattainable for you. Knowing that it is always inside and your outer focus from fear is the only barrier to your achieving this delight is the secret to life and your feelings of success.

Happiness is the experience of joy, contentment, and well-being, combined with a sense that one's life is good, meaningful, successful and worthwhile. The feeling of happiness is achieved by following one's heart and doing what brings you joy. There are many ways for one to train the mind to achieve happiness. Choose loving thoughts, words, and actions in every situation you encounter throughout your day. The more you cultivate your inner knowing through love, compassion, and observation, the more you become a vibrant source of happiness that radiates outwardly to others.

It is in one's innermost essence of divine connection that joy and happiness naturally arise. Most people call this experience, God. Experiencing happiness is about looking deeply within to see which action brings true happiness and which to eliminate because of suffering. Happiness requires discipline and effort but when you are nourished by happiness, exercising discipline becomes a joyful action that brings you more calmness, clarity, contentment and insight. It is treasuring every moment of life.

You feel better and more of the things that you want will flow to you. No one is keeping score. Your tasks will never be all done. Realize that you will never have everything you want to satisfy you. This unfinished place is the best space that you can be. You are right on track, right on schedule.

The best is yet to come. Well being is flowing to you. Everything is unfolding perfectly. Life is supposed to be fun. Have fun! Join me on this new highway as we grow into love's oneness with harmony, balance, and bliss. Success is no longer hidden!

This is the path of the masters. The masters stress the liberating impact of realizing this truth. To realize God, to know your true identity, to become enlightened is why we descended and now climb back up Jacob's Ladder of consciousness, the spiritual ascension. It is the goal that we seek. Master Beinsa Douno says, "When … you find God, you will find yourself as well. When you see God, you will see yourself. To see God and to see yourself — that is the most sacred moment in life. Man lives for that very moment."

It is in that sacred moment that the ego defers to the Father, leaving only Him. In that moment, form becomes formlessness and God meets God. This is true success.

Luminary Light

By Marilyn L. Redmond

Darkness is all I know,
depression saturates my soul.
Difficulties abound
like plowing through snow mounds.
No light to show the way,
only troubles, misery are at bay.
Searching everyday for answers to understand
floundering in a storm, seeing others on shores stand.

Prayers seem unanswered-only grief,
begging brings no relief.
Drowning in a sea of fear,
please throw a life ring near.
How do you survive the waves of despair
is anyone really there or cares?
Desperately hanging on tossing through rainy weather,
a bit of sun shines through like a tether.

This glimmer brings hope at last
maybe the worst has past.
Little by little, light shines more
so I can better see the shore.
Struggles continue, anxiety is strong,
oh where, oh where did I go wrong?
Dark clouds gradually move away
I long for more light to stay.

Finally, my steps are on solid ground,
my journey is homeward bound.
Small steps smoothly move me forward,
new guidance emerges and is heard.
Daily the game plays out repeatedly,
this chess game moves on continually.
Times of struggle interfere with progress
how will I ever resolve this dreadful mess?

How long does it take to forgive the perils
that felt like climbing over barrels?
Can accepting I created this script
bring peace when the plan is ripped?
A choice to surrender is humility
or continue in ego's force is sterility.
There is a choice for love, to thrive
Or pursuing personal pursuits and die.

Only when love fills my soul
Opens my heart, then I am bold.
In the light of day I clearly see
what lies ahead for me.
It goes before me to smooth my path,
forgiveness, compassion dissolves my wrath.
Be love for that is what you are.
God is patient, it's my star.   © 2014

Chapter Three

I Wanted to Live

As I am peering downward to planet Earth, God asks me, *Do you really want to go down and help those people that are unhappy and suffering?* I was told, that *You cannot help them unless you also experience what they experience.* I seemed to have no choice but to move forward, embracing the mystery of life, so I can understand the universal dynamics that provide the basis for our lives. My fate included the great loss of not receiving parental love and nurturing while transforming my life to achieving love for myself and offering missing care and fostering of love to others. My story does not begin as a sweet, loved baby girl. I felt my mother's fear in the womb.

I survived through many life-altering events from abuse in infancy, throughout childhood, and marriage to know which solutions will help me move beyond past fears, and problems while healing mental illness and many diseases. Healing nine addictions and various abuses in childhood and a thirty-year marriage of domestic violence of rape, has brought wisdom. In addition, I was born with my parents' fear and karma to heal.

My life as Cinderella was hopeless. I encourage you to accept the challenge into maturity. If I can change *"existing in hell"* to thriving in "heaven on earth" — living in Christ-consciousness — anyone can! **Leave** your chrysalis behind and grow into an incredible and beautiful butterfly — free in reality.

My story can help uncover answers to restore well being. Finding and understanding the obstacles to a healthy life brings empowerment, understanding, and wisdom, emerging from *"victim to victor."*

I always felt like an orphan from the time of my birth. Feeling alone and lonely, I never believed that I fit in anywhere. Gradually, as I changed my attitude from one of fear, shock, and trauma to loving others and myself, I created a life filled with caring people and positive experiences. This spiritual shift, from fear to love, drove me to find the truth about myself.

My grandmother, Alice Reading, was born in Everett, Washington, then a small town north of Seattle. Muzzy, the name I called my grandmother, married my grandfather, a Canadian named Mr. Parker. Mother and her five sisters and two brothers were all born in Canada. My mother was born in North Battleford, Saskatchewan in 1917. My grandfather eventually abandoned the family after the birth of their eighth and youngest child, a daughter, Izola. Facing the Great Depression with a large family was a huge responsibility for anyone, especially a single mother.

How am I ever going to support my family without a husband? My girls need supervision, especially after dark if I am not home. Working long hours at the sewing factory in Seattle, Washington, she feared for their safety, especially without a man in the house. This instilled a deep fear of men within my mother. In addition, because of hard times, my mother lived with relatives several times. During high school, Mom lived in Portland, Oregon with a cousin. However, the lack of money prevented her graduation. My mother's very real fear of not having enough money because of the Great Depression haunted her. It was during this time that my parents met at a ballroom in Seattle.

At the age of twenty-two, I sat at a table with my father, husband, and baby daughter, enjoying a seafood dinner on the waterfront in Seattle. He shared his story only once. "My mother with my seven brothers and sisters left Russia one night through a swamp. My youngest brother was a baby in my mother's arms. We had to be perfectly still when the boats patrolled. Terrified, we submerged under the water with reeds to breathe through. If there were a ripple in the water, the soldiers would shoot from their patrol boats. Surviving the trauma, we then walked through two towns to get to the shore for the boat to take us to England and on to America.

"While my father was a jeweler for the Czar of Russia, he sent my father out of the country to protect him. My father sent my mother his earnings from the United States for us to join him. We moved into a house on Fir Street in Seattle. I was six years old when I began selling newspapers on the streets of Seattle to help with the family finances. Though my father had brought us to Seattle for a better life, he never lived with us again."

My mother, Mary Alice Parker, was an impressionable, flaming red-haired twenty-year-old girl when she married my forty-year-old father, Julius (Jules) Edward Markow. In the beginning, my father did not want any more children; he had a daughter from a previous marriage.

My mother wanted a child of her own. Instead of having a child, they bought a house. My mother however, was more stubborn about having a child and eventually talked my father into it. Shortly, Dad luckily changed his mind about me. In due course, I managed to become my father's little princess and my mother's little doll.

However, being a member of this family was not fun and I never felt safe. Every night was the same. *I wish they would stop fighting;* I wanted a happy family. As a three-year-old, I did not have the words, but I tried never to think about it and would pretend it never happened. Denial of reality ran my life.

Mom accidentally left the door open to my room one night and I saw my father beat my mother in our tiny bathroom. My mother screaming, "I have no money to buy groceries." It felt like he was beating me, too. I thought, *If he can't see me, he can't hurt me.* My inner voice went on, *If I have enough money, I will make it.* This inner voice spoke to me at crucial times over the years. My father, though very stingy with the grocery money, supported his little princess in her dancing and performing. I did not know it at the time that some of these lessons were also paid out of my mother's household money.

Mom made colorful costumes for my solo tap and ballet dances and outfits for other dancers in my classes. She applied my makeup for the performances in the cold, bare cement dressing rooms back stage of the Moore Theater. My mother lived through me; I was her doll. She always dressed me up for dancing, school, and church. "I love the costumes and clothes your mother makes you," my neighbor girl, Gloria, told me.

One warm summer afternoon, I was looking up into the blue sky at the cloud formations. They fascinated me. Mom called out from a window, "If you do not have something to do, I can find something for you to do." I went into the house as requested and never had a spare moment after that.

My older half sister, Vickie, came from Canada to live with us when I started kindergarten. After her high school graduation, she went to work at Boeing Airplane Company. After dating just a short time, Vickie became engaged. The engagement party was a fun time at our home, everyone singing by the piano to the new Cole Porter song, *"Night and Day."* I wanted to be part of the only time there was laughter in our house. "Mom, I want to stay up and have fun, too."

"This is an adult party," she told me.

A short time later, for one of the few times in my life, I tried talking to Mom. I wanted to tell her my feelings about the incest from my soon to be brother-in-law, during the party. I quickly discovered that my mother was not available to help me in any way.

Vickie's marriage became a battering, abusive, and an alcoholic disaster. It was a re-creation of my parents' marriage and later my own marriage. Later, Mom told me, "I have to go to work as your father will not give me enough money for food. You will not be able to continue your dancing lessons." The disappointment from this announcement was crushing; dancing was the only place I felt good and safe. In addition, we lost touch with our friends from the dancing studio. I looked forward to those times for lunches and many afternoons at their pleasant homes.

I found out my father drank because well-meaning neighbors always kept Mom informed. My father never drank at home. Though Dad came home most nights, he rarely stayed there. Many nights he came home already having had a few drinks. If he did not like the dinner my mother had prepared, he picked a fight and would leave for a nearby restaurant. In later years, my father did stop drinking and became a generous, devoted grandfather.

Mom and I had been going to the nearest church from the time I was old enough to walk there with her. Mom found strength in the course of her job as a bank teller. She talked to our minister about getting a divorce. Our church, Missouri Synod Lutheran, did not believe in divorce at that time; however, Mom was able to carry through and separate from my father.

My parents' divorce took place when I was eight years old. My father never said "good-bye." Never having communications, I began to read voraciously, looking to quench my insatiable thirst for help and answers.

Mom met my step-dad at a dance at the Trianon Ballroom in Seattle. My father had allowed Mom and me to remain in our residence at Green Lake in Seattle until she remarried. Mom's experience with my father extended into her second marriage. Again, it was an incompatible mixture with addictions, mental illness, and dysfunction.

He went for neighborhood walks to cool down just like my father. At his mother's house for Christmas the first year, my step-dad gave me some instructions for chores at home the next day. I had a question that was minor; however, I was told, "Never talk back to your elders," as he slapped me in the face.

After her second marriage, Mom began suffering chronic illnesses. Shortly after my younger half sister was born, his mother, who was a bitter woman, told me that she would never treat me like a granddaughter because I was not of her blood. Her new granddaughter was her only granddaughter.

I was continually waiting for the other shoe to drop, as if I were walking through a mine field all the time at home. Arriving home from high school one afternoon, I was surprised that my step-dad was not at work. He showed me pictures from a magazine of private parts. Out of a clear blue sky at dinner one evening, he announced, "What happens at home stays at home and what you learn at church stays at church."

Even with all my reading, I never found the answers to why my life was so scary and unhappy. I never felt safe. Because graduating from high school as valedictorian brought no recognition or value at home, I believed graduating from college *cum laude* would finally bring me acknowledgment. "We never got you a graduation gift from college, did we?" my step-dad said thirty years after I had graduated. My parents never spoke a word of praise after I soloed with the Bellingham Symphony, either.

My husband and I met at a college dance, called a "mixer." He took me home after the dance. We dated off and on for three years. I wanted out of our engagement when his anger became a problem. However, I found myself pregnant. I married to be acceptable in the fifties. With our busy schedules, the only time we could hold the wedding was the Saturday after winter finals in our senior year. After the weekend, we were off on tour with the college band.

My marriage to Prince Charming took place as designed. I walked down the aisle planning on a divorce. Somehow, I knew this was not to be a happy marriage. Six months into our marriage, he strangled and raped me when I said "No" to sex that night. "I am too tired from taking care of our daughter," I replied. We pretended this incident never happened and went on with our lives as if nothing had changed. We built our lovely home after we both graduated as teachers from college. Throughout the marriage, he bought me sexy clothes to turn him on. I thought this meant that he loved me.

My husband always drank from the time I knew him. Unfortunately, he would drink until he got drunk, boisterous, and irrational. Years later, I learned about his father's alcoholism, his mother's total lack of emotional availability, mental illness, and their domestic violent marriage. It was a total match to my family.

Our son was born five years later. When our children were still young, we frequently took them on family trips during school vacations. My mother kept laying guilt trips on me for not being at every occasion, even a family dinner. My mother and husband detested each other and both demanded my loyalty; therefore, he decided we would take trips over the holidays. On our first trip to Disneyland at Christmas time, we found a motel room close to the amusement park. "I want to go for a drink," he powerfully told me. "Are you coming with me?"

I responded, "But the children have not had dinner." However, I was afraid of his hurting me if I did not go with him. Therefore, I left the children in a strange motel in an unfamiliar town and went with him.

Our odyssey of doctors and drugs began as a direct result of my mother's mental and physical illnesses. At a family dinner, my stepfather asked for help from my husband and me. Because of her threat of suicide, I placed her in the hospital where she received shock treatments. The doctor said, "It is a miracle that she can go home and live a fairly normal existence." At the time, my step-dad never revealed the diagnosis of paranoid-schizo-phrenia.

After a short time, my husband's temper and rage actually increased. This created more tension and anxiety for the family and me. Mom's doctor gave him a prescription for Valium. This brought more of his temper tantrums and anxiety. I needed help to cope.

I found a psychiatrist who prescribed Valium for me. For the next month, I never felt better. For the first time, I felt like I was a real person and had a life. I had a sense of self-esteem that I had never experienced before. My depression left and life seemed uniquely happy. However, over time, my moods became more and more depressing until I tried suicide several times. Ultimately, I became addicted. I learned in treatment that a combination of one pill and one drink creates six times the effect of a single medication or drink.

No matter how clean the house, no matter how weed-free or perfect the yard, and vegetable garden, I never knew when he would start screaming at me and chase me through the house. Only one time I tried to get help from the police, but that was to no avail in the 70's.

My façade of smiles while teaching at local grade schools and junior high school crowned my deep-seated core problems. Imitations of social graces from dancing lessons, musical performances, church activities, and college helped my adult-like appearance camouflage my inner pain. Singing in the church choir and teaching Vacation Bible School masked the overwhelming anxiety that never left.

My husband was wonderful to his friends but not to me. I exhausted myself working so hard, trying to make him and everyone else happy and never quite succeeding. In speaking with my daughter on the phone when I left him for a short time, because he was threatening to kill me, she exclaimed, "Mom, he's always threatening to kill you."

Then one night, my husband's rage about our son and me watching television, which was disturbing him in another room, escalated out of control. Returning home to eat Thanksgiving dinner, I dropped my fork and left this time with the intention of never returning; I could not endure it anymore. I kept leaving through the day to escape his wrath; I returned, this time actually planning to take my cache of pills.

Angels appeared and had me stop taking the pills. I returned home to his raging and was in a fog for several years. After another tirade, he told me, "If you are not moved out by the end of the teaching year, I will kill you." I left quickly that day.

We agreed to stop drinking for three weeks. To celebrate our newfound sobriety, he suggested a trip. He wanted to reconcile our marriage.

We enjoyed golfing at our favorite getaway place in Canada, Harrison Hot Springs. After his first drink of celebration before coming home from a lovely time, he went into a fury because I had pinned up the front of my dress. I was humiliated as his wrath continued through dinner and dancing in the Copper Room of the hotel. He ranted, "I am leaving, and if you go with me, you are not to get out of the car until we get home." I could not stay in Canada as I felt like a child being abandoned in a foreign country. In high anxiety, I was in a car moving across the center lane back and forth at a high speed. We nearly missed two head-on collisions. I was terrified and prayed, "God, please help me, I really don't want to die." For the first time, I realized that I wanted to live. Thank God, there was very little traffic at 2:00 am.

Five police cars responded to my message I left at a coffee shop for help. One officer escorted me to a police car, as my husband sat silently in our car, removing the grocery money from my purse that he had given me the night before at dinner. "We've never had a situation like this before," the police officers said.

My husband found a 12-step program called AA; he encouraged me to attend Al-Anon. Divorce papers and a restraining order had forced him to examine his life, seriously. My husband and I separated for more short periods several times. Each time we got back together, I felt stronger and more confident from my meetings and counseling as I was learning to be on my own.

As I began to understand my parents' fears, it brought

clarity to the nightmarish fantasy that drove my life. Realizing my problems were a continuation of my family dynamics, I knew I had to change my inner foundation.

Our family looked normal in our community. Our children were confirmed in the church. We paid our bills on time. Our exotic trips to places like Hawaii, Mexico, and the Bahamas covered deep inner pain and misery that we never showed to the world. Along with my teaching school and teaching flute lessons, I returned to school to achieve seven years of college while I continued working in the family printing business and attending all my children's events and activities.

Finally, I found the missing information for changing my life. I had deceived myself because I did not realize life is lived on two planes. I thought life went well, if you looked good and did the right things. I lived in the created illusion of perfection, so totally perfected, that my neighbor told me after the divorce, "I thought you had the perfect marriage." I knew, however, my life was not that way. I felt like the walking dead. I did not know there were spiritual laws of the universe and a loving higher power.

I realized one day that if I did not change my part of the dynamics, I would re-create the same dysfunctional marriage with a new spouse. With my genetic history, dysfunctional family, and past life issues called karma, the future had been determined. However, if I changed me, I could change my life.

I understood for the first time the problem. There was an unspoken law of *no talk, no trust, and no feelings* in our family. Using alcohol for courage was my way to handle life. Alcohol made be brave. Pills took away the anxiety; they gave me patience. I had no life skills; I had never grown up; I was emotionally stuck at the age of three from witnessing the traumatic fights of my parents.

I found other addictions like smoking, sugar, workaholism, overachieving, and depending on my husband and family members, called co-dependency, were all needing to be healed with a loving Father of the Universe. I could substitute and respond in a positive or loving attitude, action, or communication. This allowed the cause to change for a better result. It was about cause and effect. I had to accept the reality of love to find happiness.

I had run away from reality in my fear, because I was afraid of love. I could turn this around and trust a loving universe to support me in all things. That love within my heart can now open to love others as I love myself.

I have released the old emotions with loving solutions. Through many hypnosis regressions and meditation, I have healed my soul into a whole spirit—holy spirit. Most people on the spiritual path ignore healing the subconscious that is the basis for our lives. Today I am fearless. One of my biggest fears was abandonment. What is your unfinished business?

Recently, the universe tested my abandonment issue. An acquaintance told me that my man friend was seen with a beautiful woman several times. At first I was surprised, as we are in contact every day or together. Then, my ego went to work and the feelings of abandonment surfaced.

However, quickly, I started identifying how much he has helped me with his Pranic healing work for my health problems. He accepts me unconditionally and I am able to be myself, today. Through his 15 years of loyal support, I have grown up. If he was going on another path, I realized how much I had benefited from our association. I would not lose my self worth or life, if he left.

When I arrived home a couple of hours later, he called. I was able to ask him, "Are you seeing another woman?" Immediately his reaction told me he was not in any way involved in such a thing. "I do not even like that restaurant they said I was leaving," he responded robustly. This incident actually brought us closer together. He became more attentive.

I have discovered my tasks will never be all done. I am right on track, right on schedule. Everything is unfolding perfectly. There will be challenges to continue the choice to respond in love to all my experiences.

The secret in life is attracting higher vibrations of love. When I released the negative emotional basis from my past, I had an inner void. The silent voice inside told me that now I could fill that void with self-esteem. Each time I let go of another fault, I was told to replace it with love and grace. I will never forget the first time I felt grace. Today, I know I am a spiritual being releasing my human shortcomings.

I became a love-based person instead of a fear-based person. To improve my surroundings, I try to focus upon the best things currently around me until I flood my vibrational patterns with thoughts of appreciation and/or faith.

Early in recovery, I started a gratitude list that I add to daily to keep my focus on thankfulness. I had to lift my self-imposed limitations—all limitations are self-imposed—and free myself to receive wonderful things. With a changed higher vibration, I allow the new-and-improved conditions and circumstances to come into my experience.

Ask yourself, "What do I want?" Take one of your wants and ask yourself the following questions: What feelings will I have if I want more, get that, or want what I do not have today? How will I change when I get this want? How will my life change when I get this want? What do I see my life looking like when

I get this want?

In the moment, with my new state of being vibrating my own unique vibration, with no agendas or planning, I create my new life by attracting like energies in perfect synchronicity and timing. No one can deny or grant anything. I attract it by vibration. It is a universal law that *like attracts like*.

When I understand this principle, it became easy to differentiate between what raises my vibrations closer to my Creator and what keeps me separated. **I found I could** raise my energy by using tuning forks, receiving energy work, getting acupuncture, and by means of massage. In addition, applying principles, prayer, and meditation will raise my energy into a higher consciousness.

Other means include taking homeopathic remedies as flower essences, Chinese herbs, and drinking pure water support a higher energy within. Watching spiritual movies, reading spiritual material and listening to classical music raise my spirit. In addition, consuming non-toxic drinks, eating organic foods, and looking for the good in my life make a big change.

The following quote by Benjamin Franklin sums it up: "Through what seemed like insurmountable obstacles, persistently reaching for the better thought, for authenticity and trust brought me to a place of abundance, self-acceptance and love. Of course, the journey continues with new seeds of awareness sprouting every day. Using our God-given energy to persist in love we can face the monsters and live to tell the tale. Even transform them into beautiful beings of light. It's what we all signed up for."

My life today is not without tests and challenges. I do not put myself in places to be hurt and my past is not being re-created in my life. Gratefully, my fear of financial insecurity has left. I can even speak up today when intimidated and in tough situations.

My biggest learning has been to meditate. Listening to my inner guidance and direction has brought me the truth for which I was searching. I know that my spiritual help is with me constantly for support and protection. I am empowered. I have learned to respond in love instead of react in fear. My third-dimensional life of duality based in fear has moved into the reality of "oneness" where there is peace, harmony, and balance —a higher consciousness.

In the last thirty years, I have overcome nine addictions including several co-dependencies, mental illness, PTSD, domestic violence, depression, pneumonia, Fibromyalgia, anxiety, and more. I have learned how the dynamics of life work and how to change the cause and consequences in life to feel better. I have awakened into a higher consciousness in fifth dimension.

Life is about becoming mature. I create my own reality. When I changed, my life changed. I found the light inside. That light within is the creator and in all things. It is my power, strength, and supply. The spiritual core of my enlightenment emerges as the darkness leaves. My assignment is to share my answers and solutions.

My tasks will never be all done. Now, I realize that I will never have everything I want to satisfy me. This unfinished place is the best space that I can be. I am right on track, right on schedule. I will feel better and I will find more of the things that I want flow to me. No one is keeping score. Are you having fun yet? The best is yet to come.

The time to be ME is now. I live in the "Now." I am healthier today than I ever have been. I am courageous and no longer a victim. My life is no longer chaotic, in turmoil, or threatening. It feels like heaven on earth with peace of mind and prosperity.

I am able to honestly communicate my needs, share my feelings, and trust a higher power. For many years, I have been in a healthy liaison of unconditional love. I am in joy, with gratitude and in the presence of love.

I can allow the achievement of anything that I desire be considered success, whether it is an award, money, relationships, or good feelings. My standard of success is my achievement of joy. Then everything else will fall easily into place. For in experiencing joy, I find vibrational alignment with the treasures of the Universe.

The good part of this means God's love is reality. I had run away from reality because I was afraid of love. Now, I can trust a God who loves me, instead of looking to untrustworthy parents or an abusive husband. Trust in a higher power gave me the ability to communicate my needs, feelings and be myself. I am happy, joyous and free. I found "joyful acceptance" in all parts of my life. Life is good. Life is love. That love within my heart can now completely open to love others as I love myself. Everything is unfolding perfectly. Life is to enjoy! I share my answers and solutions.

Life is Love: Affirmations for Living

By Marilyn Redmond

It is okay to be one with God!
It's okay to feel good.
It's okay to enjoy love.
It's okay to share love.
It's okay to move in love.
It's okay to express love.
It's okay to experience love.
It's okay to be filled with love.
It's okay to allow love to flow in my life.
It's okay to have love flow through me, for my health.
It's okay to have love nurture me.
It's okay to thrive in love.
It's okay to create in love.
It's okay to allow love.
It's okay to live in love.
It's okay to give love.
It's okay to be love.
It's okay to accept the great present of love.   © 2014

Chapter Four

Love Never Fails

Life Did Not Go My Way

My life was unmanageable. I married, thinking I could improve my life and create a happier family. I found later that the family I created felt familiar. The alcoholism, codependency, and mental illness were still very much alive. My life had the same problems that I was trying to escape. If I can transform my life, anyone can.

Growing up, I tried to be accepted by my family by earning honors as being valedictorian, recognition when soloing with the Bellingham Symphony, and acknowledgement as an excellent teacher. With my long list of achievements, my family never did praise or congratulate me for all my hard work or completing seven years of college. In fact, these outer successes did not provide the missing feelings of being fulfilled, loved, and safe.

I had nothing to lose by trying something different. A common explanation of insanity is doing the same thing repeatedly and expecting different results. My plan was to create the happy family. I was tired from my determined efforts. At first, it was difficult to realize that my trying so hard to have a cheerful and positive family was not working. When trying to set the stage for a great outcome and to be safe, things seemed to fall apart. Life did not turn out as I envisioned and tried earnestly to work out. After 30 years in domestic violence, this was not happening.

Looking for new answers for life became imperative in my situation. I tried suicide and my husband tried to kill me several times. After years of misery and unhappiness, I finally had to find answers. When it became a matter of life and death, ultimately, I prayed, "God please help me, I really don't want to die."

I was naïve thinking my prayer would not be answered. My discomfort brought me to a turning point, where I was willing to be open to new ways of thinking and handling my life. In fact, new opportunities came quickly. Promptly, I found myself in counseling, support groups, and classes to help find healthy information for my life. I wanted to be at ease instead of always in anxiety and fear. I guardedly tried these new ways that appeared seemly out of nowhere. The crisis, chaos, and turmoil in my life were like a hurricane. Moving into the "eye of the hurricane," where there is peace and calmness, sounded wonderful to me.

In childhood, my information came from family, friends, and religion. I listened to the doctors and ministers and more problems multiplied. I became addicted from doctors' prescriptions and my minster thought I should stay in my tormenting marriage. I did not find my answers in reading autobiographies, either. I read every one I could, looking for how famous people arranged their lives.

I was a sponge and followed my parents' lead. However, it was not working for me. At that time, I did not understand that people pass down what they learn without question and keep perpetuating what does not work. My family modeled their beliefs and mind-set. Learning that I could create my own mind-set to overcome my inherited genetics, not volunteer to be a victim, and release all false beliefs brought freedom.

My head was programmed from my parents' and society's fears that produced hopelessness and helplessness. I know today, old information and learning usually comes from the left-brain from which the ego sends negative messages. I thoroughly believed those mental comments, as *I am not good enough,* or that *I deserve to be hurt if my mother is hurt every night.* Some people describe the ego as "Edging God out." In addition, reacting was typical as I learned it well. Experiencing and witnessing abusive experiences resulted in my reenacting survival automatically.

My prayer was the first time that I turned to an inner message from my spirit for answers and help. Accessing my inner direction and guidance from my heart was foreign to me. My church preached against meditation and listening to the voice within; therefore it was scary to try this new approach. However, my first prayer brought great results. Trusting to access the right side of the brain as a connection to a loving source that wants goodness for me was novel.

Turning inside for direction was a huge leap in faith. My new life was going to become a walk in faith rather than listening to those around me. I could choose listening to loving messages instead of my head. I could substitute positive for negative. Gradually, I found relief, moments of serenity, and a beginning to understand myself. I realized that I acted out looking for security and love in my life. Ultimately, I had been trying to compensate for missing support, caring, and affection.

I was taught to use others to make me okay, care for me, and provide my protection. My mother married during the Depression. She met my father at a dance. I believe she married him because he had a job, which became her security. I was addicted, called codependency, to those people that could not be there for themselves. It was a losing illusion. Learning later that I had to be responsible for my own needs was a new shift in reality, again.

I did not see that my addictions kept me a victim and immature. They actually made my desperation more intense over time. I discovered that addictions support this lack of reality. Drinking, prescriptions, and smoking cigarettes kept me in my fantasy that others were there for me and would take care of me. Addictions stop emotional growth and a connection to a loving higher power. I had not grown up emotionally to take responsibility for my life.

Learning that I can find contentment, happiness, and good health through new attitudes, open-mindedness and honesty, with the willingness to walk a new path of faith was the answer for which I was searching. What harm can a new perspective do? If nothing changes, nothing changes. I could learn to love myself and apply positive thinking in my adventure. I could create a change in my life by being responsible while growing in self-esteem.

How Do I Begin?

Some people say denial is lying to yourself and not even knowing you are doing it. I was protecting myself in my Cinderella existence. I lived for most of my life with my head in the sand as a good ostrich doing what I was told. In addition, while growing up, I listened to a radio show called, "Let's Pretend." Later, I pretended I was in a wonderful marriage with two lovely children. I looked good teaching, attending church, and socializing. This was a psychological way to ignore my early abuse. However, this denial kept me immobilized, desperate, and powerless throughout my life. Realizing that I had to face the facts about circumstances and myself was shocking.

Coming out of denial means being honest with myself. I lived in mental illness and delusion. That is insanity. Learning that a power greater than myself could restore my thinking to sanity was a novel idea. Waking up to see what I did not see before made the difference. I had not been truthful with myself.

How can I be insane? I always have good grades in school. My façade at work seemed to be working. I have a clean home. My bills are paid. Our family takes lovely trips even out of the country to places like Canada, the Bahamas, and Mexico.

It took a while to understand that when I am not honest, I do not connect with the real world. I researched paranoid schizophrenia when I heard that my mother was diagnosed with that label. I found that mentally ill people are not honest with themselves. Dr. Peck in his book, *People of the Lie*, said that the degree of dishonesty with self is the determination for each level of mental illness. I vowed to be as honest with myself as I possibly could.

Learning about cause and effect brought new understanding. I did not want to be mentally ill like my mother. When I react from fear, I am not rational. I will not get rational results. It is the negative thinking, behaviors, and actions that created more negativity that created my misery and pain.

"You cannot be your own guide out of the problems that your blind spots have created. Only Your Creator can do this," according to Ernest F. Pecci, M.D.

Maybe, a new positive basis for my life and actions would bring helpful outcomes. Becoming honest and seeing the good in life was necessary for sanity. Over time, my new foundation was fruitfully evolving. However, new problems would arise and I needed more tools to help me keep my focus on the solution. When I heard no one is where he is by accident and chance plays no part in the plan of the Cosmos, I began to see I had to take the reins of my life.

Affirmations became a major focal point. I acquired a list of affirmations for self-love. I had never affirmed myself nor had anyone in my life. I started repeating them daily. I needed to find self-esteem. Affirmations gave me permission to acknowledge and praise myself verbally. Some of these affirmations are: *I approve of all my actions. I am confident in my ability. I give myself pleasure without guilt. I love my body and see only its good qualities. I give myself what I want and what I need. I let myself win.*

Over the years new affirmations surfaced that met my current needs to confirm my worth.

I found flower essences supported this change into loving energy. I particularly liked two different companies: The Bach and Tree Frog Farm flower essences were especially helpful. I found that Bach essences were helpful for changing basic emotions and the Tree Frog Farm ones supported spiritual growth. Together they work well for me.

This was the beginning of my new path and lifestyle. I take the pure energy of the flower essences daily and tell myself the compatible affirmations to support the releasing of the old toxic, negative energy. The new higher energy replaces the old lower vibrations of energy.

More Steps to Change

I had self-created survival mechanisms masking my insecurity and inadequacy. What would become of me if my survival mechanisms were questioned and changed? I wore a mask to show the world that I was okay. Nevertheless, it became basic to identify which parts of my life did not work. Discovering my identity was connected to my lack of feeling safe, unworthy, and poor health was important. Could I release those for a better self-image of me?

My mother received her validation by being sick. My father was an alcoholic. My wanting to leave this kind of basis for my worth and recognition was necessary. Does a hereditary condition need be a lifelong sentence? Must I accept every medical diagnosis and live the rest of my life with the diagnosis? I found that I did not have to live the life of my mother or father. I can have my own mind-set and think for myself.

In addition, I could release the past and not keep re-creating it. This pain became so overwhelming, I knew something had to change. It was time for guidance to thaw toxic old emotions from my past so they can be released. I found happy feelings came in to replace the old feelings. This makes the journey worth the effort. As it says on the first page of *A Course In Miracles*, "Miracles are natural. When they do not occur, something has gone wrong."

Going to church was important to my family. I saw that what was said from the pulpit was not what I read in the Bible. This was frustrating. The messages did not match. I heard dogma from the minister and love from the Bible. Are my beliefs based in truth? What is the truth?

With my inquiring mind, I began my search for reality.

Several spiritual groups helped me find a path that was spiritual instead of religious. I was eager to learn. Becoming open-minded and accepting new ideas was exciting. After a time I was thrilled to see that I finally was on the path that worked for me.

Years later, I realized that my early resistance to change actually brought my pain and misery. Being afraid of the unknown is typical; however, I was eager to move forward now. Because I wanted a better life, I took action to start the changes no matter how fearful I felt. I am still out of my comfort zone when growing into new places. I know today, that all things work for good if you are on the path of love. Today, I am on an adventure; this interpretation seems to lower my apprehension.

Astonishingly, information came at the right times. I have learned to think of it as a journey to learn about myself and the world I can create. Information and awareness gave me the motivation to move from my old ways into a new lifestyle. In addition, I found other people in my support group moving forward in their lives, too. It is true that once the student is willing, the teacher will appear.

Through teachings of institutions such as schools, health organizations, governmental laws and regulations, society and even churches, we are led down a path that is not of our choosing. We become like puppets and all of these institutions pull our strings without our even realizing it. We are like lemmings, doomed conformists, blindly following one another on a course. We are indoctrinated to believe that all of these institutions have the right answers and we do not question them, as we might.

How do I continue my launching forward? The first phase is to admit that there is a problem. With only the smallest desire, I could begin creating a new life. There comes a time when becoming willing or even willing to be willing, wins. Truth is the most powerful element in the universe. It unlocks the door to understanding and discovering a new world. It was time to open Pandora's Box of denial so the hidden falsehoods can fly out. "Knowing the truth will set you free."

Recognition, acceptance, declaration, and demonstration are four steps into reality. Recognition of reality is a choice. Seeing the bigger picture of my life put things into perspective. It also shows me where I erred. With honesty and acceptance, I can start to rebuild a real foundation upon which to create a new life.

I was living in "silent desperation." When I acknowledge this, change happens. Cleaning out the old for new ideas to refill the space is important. A saying goes, "Love is an expression of the willingness to create space in which something is allowed to change."

Life is a Choice

The feelings and emotions that I had allowed to run my life disconnected me from belonging. When I deny myself, I deny the love within. Every time I see myself as "not good enough," in lack, or insufficiency of any kind, or not safe, I am in denial of the real me. Thinking that it is humble to deny my talents and abilities, I really deny the divinity within.

Resistance to change keeps ordinary people from questioning what we are doing. When we decide to move out of our previous thinking, we threaten the status quo. Our acceptance of the truth ends our denial. Most people are not into self-examination and inquiring. Therefore, it is significant to find people who support my new ideas and purpose. My friends and jobs changed as I grew.

I am powerless when I am in denial. When I accept everything, I can then change it. Acceptance places me in power. I am responsible for my feelings. I am responsible for my life. If I can change my beliefs, I can change my actions; therefore, I can change my feelings. Old feelings can change and pass, thereby allowing space for good feelings to fill the new void. "This too shall pass" is a popular saying.

"There are in truth no incurable conditions," said Edgar Cayce, The Father of Holistic Health. A shift in perception from fear to love — living instead of dying — made the difference. As time progressed, continuing my self-analysis became necessary to grow into maturity.

Being honest with me made it obvious that my old thinking was irrational. It had to be, how else could you justify my erratic behavior? If you read a dictionary definition of rationalization, you will find that rationalization is giving a socially acceptable reason for socially unacceptable behavior and socially unacceptable behavior is a form of insanity.

Often, though, it takes a crisis to stop and scrutinize your situation and then determine your own wisest solution. In my chaotic car ride home from Canada, I feared I would not get home alive. My terror escalated as my husband drove down the wrong side of the road at high speeds, stopping on the centerline and then moving forward again at the same velocity on both sides of the road. We almost had two head-on collisions. He was driving like a maniac. His actions were one more example of his insanity (and mine as well). Instinctively, I knew I had to take some action. This crisis precipitated my cry for help. I realized at last that I had to break the cycle of constant turmoil that predominated our lives.

It was time to choose a loving spirit of the universe for my focus and care. Relying on spiritual support instead of people, places, and material things, including money, brought strength, and consistency upon which I could finally build a real life.

Surprisingly, my new path appeared. I found a sincere desire for open-mindedness, honesty, and willingness to change. I had been spiritually bankrupt and now I wanted a conscious connection to my higher power. Now I know the highest desire of the soul is to experience unconditional love, *the presence of God.* As human beings, we frequently do not think that we are loved. These old feelings and emotions get in the way of accepting our inheritance of unconditional love. Today, feelings are a guide and feedback, so I can course correct my life and feel good. Love never fails.

About Fear

Fear is the basis of all negative feelings. Recognizing that my life was a reaction to fear was a shock. I was walking fear, guilt, and shame. Learning that I was self-centered and selfish from my survival instincts did make sense. Learning that fear could be interpreted as "False Emotions Appearing Real" helped me dispel fears as I began my spiritual journey. My new commitment to become a love-based person became an intense declaration.

Staying in fear is hazardous. Typically, fear is feedback to inform you to move into a loving perception of faith, acceptance, or gratitude. Fear can be feeling terrified of speaking in front of a group or not being able to get in a car unless you are the one driving. The goal is to discern the kind of fear you are feeling at any given time and to act accordingly.

There are a few more steps to take to make it possible to be in alignment with the universe. This is an inside job. Now understanding that nothing outside me can save me or give me peace,

I needed to turn within. *A Course in Miracles* T. 315 says, "Your task is not to seek for love, but merely to seek and find all the barriers within yourself that you have built against it. It is not necessary to seek for what is true, but it <u>is</u> necessary to seek for what is false."

My next course of action was to identify all my fears, one by one, along with all my resentments and behaviors that came from my fears. Where was I selfish, dishonest, frightened, or inconsiderate? Whom had I harmed?

Fear causes us to "react." This means giving away my power by believing the fear has influence over me. This creates the victim mentality. The result is a loss of self-esteem, feeling hopeless and helpless. When I realize that love has power and that fear is powerless, I find a constructive solution. I can move beyond and the fear leaves.

Matthew of the Bible explained fear from his channeling through his mother, Suzy Ward:

"The energy of fear forms a barrier between the feared object or circumstances and the energy of light. Because of the barrier, the light in the souls of fear-full people cannot reach their consciousness to dispel the power of those fears over their lives, and the light being sent to them by light workers cannot penetrate.

"The barrier feels like a real wall, isolating the person with the consuming fear and leaving no way out. This energy blockage of the light intensifies the power of whatever is feared, thus enabling it to draw to itself more manifestations to be feared. Fear is wildly contagious, and due to its magnification in power, fear sensation streamers have sticky edges that attract the kinds of energetic interactions that omit common sense, sound judgment, and wise decisions.

"Fear is so insidious that it can convince a person that the only way to escape is through portals leading deeper and deeper into darkness. Fear is the forebear of such actions or characteristics deemed prejudice, tyranny, greed, cruelty, belligerence, deception, dishonor, and hatred, and even those seemingly senseless tortures or deaths of innocents arise through psyches that have been twisted and tormented by fears.

"The light, in which love and universal knowledge and spiritual clarity abide, cannot reach those souls to let them know their spiritual powers are far stronger than anything the dark powers can conjure to frighten them. Nothing is stronger than the light, which is the gift to every soul of the love and power of God." Matthew's messages are posted on www.matthewbooks.com

When I was substitute teaching in a classroom one day, we were studying the "Weekly Reader Newspaper." On the front page was a chart of the ages that you outgrow different fears. Have you outgrown your fears yet? I cannot have fear and faith at the same time. Nowadays, I choose faith daily. If I can grow up, so can you.

Another way to view fear is "a lack of information." Herbert Spencer, one of the most discussed Victorian thinkers, once said, "There is a principle which is a bar against all information, which is proof against all arguments and which cannot fail to keep a man in everlasting ignorance, — that principle is contempt prior to investigation." When you gather the data and get good information, the fear dissipates. It is said that to be well informed is to have the world at your fingers. Knowledge is empowering.

About Resentments

When I was fearful, I tried to arrange my life and the life of others. However, my resentments were also an obstacle to my prosperity and new life. Listing them and seeing how staying angry with others gave them power over me. I was reacting and staying a victim. I had to see that these people or situations were dominating my life.

It was time to realize that anger came from my perception. I could see myself angry because I was not getting my way. I did not like the way others were acting or living their lives. Moreover, I was not happy about the way my life was going. It became necessary to accept people and situations the way they are. They are living their lives as they choose. It is not my responsibility to direct their lives for my benefit. The resentment was like a temper tantrum. This is immaturity.

Accepting people, places and things as they are, is not always easy, and I did not have to like the way it was. I just had to accept the reality of it and grow up. That I had to accept life as it happens and not the way I want was a new idea. I need to meet life on life's terms and move ahead.

Interestingly, after taking an inventory of my interactions with others, I found I was inconsiderate of myself, by playing victim to all these old immature ideas. Releasing them, making amends where appropriate and forgiving them and myself was important. Then the past would no longer be the motivation of my actions.

Finding a person who understands my spiritual path can help me sort out the truth from the false in my fears, resentments, and behaviors. Their wisdom and experience helps me resolve the past that produced the fears and angers. I gain a new perception and feel like I can master my emotions instead of reacting from them. I then can let go of them and replace that space with love and grace. I have created a new foundation for my new life. I respond in love for all circumstances and situations. I created these situations for my growth. I take responsibility for them, today.

A New Basis

Through faith and truth, it is possible to rise above the fear and live beyond its influence in faith. As fear is outgrown, maturity develops. This is time to seek a spiritual counselor or someone who can help restore your total well being and living in the "Now." Being fearless brings maturity, unconditional love, and Christ Consciousness.

When turning my life over to a Creative Intelligence, a Spirit of the Universe underlying the totality of things, I felt a new power and direction to continue in my spiritual journey. My walk in faith moves me further from the fears of the past. I yield to being in the presence of peace.

I had to surrender to a loving guidance and direction from the love within my heart. I believe submitting to a loving basis for my life was the most difficult decision and action I have taken. I was giving up being the director of my life. However, replacing it to become an agent of love is powerful. Love had always been there, I was afraid to listen and be vulnerable. This was the turning point in my life.

What Stops Me from Starting?

Maybe you are thinking, will people like the real me if I change? Telling the truth can be scary. Can I tell my secrets without losing my family and friends? Can I trust others with my secrets? How will my life be different? Will I even have a life? Shouldn't my will power be enough to maintain a good life? If I look good on the outside, won't that make me change on the inside? All of these questions keep me from change.

A story most people know is Pinocchio. This story symbolizes our journey. When Pinocchio goes to Pleasure Island for all the fun and gratification, he turns into a donkey feeling despair and guilt. It is through saving his father that he loses the tail and ears from his decadent life and becomes a real boy. He became selfless in rescuing his father, Geppetto. His arrogance left in his selfless act. He became real. He found his soul by being humble, getting out of "self." When your spirit moves into wholeness, you feel complete—a whole spirit. Your needs are met. You feel good; you feel God.

It's About Vibrations of Energy

We are an energy field. It is possible to move your energy from lower energy, where there are low vibrations in selfishness, fear, and inadequacies, into higher vibrations of loving feelings. With the understanding that we are moving old energy out and that *emotions are energy in motion*, it is now possible to create the life we desire.

The universe does not know why I have a vibration. It can be from the past, what I am observing, or a memory. It just receives the vibrational energy and answers it with things that match it.

Since I cannot control circumstances, I now understand that I can control my vibrations and raise them into loving thoughts. Instead of hard work bringing me to well-being, I create through vibrations of feeling good. When I do this, I control everything around me.

I no longer need to react from the past harms, fears, or false beliefs. My new life moves into *being present* in my current experience. I had been re-creating the past as a victim of others, and now I will create a pleasant presence from my present empowerment. Moving into this new place is faith in action. I had tried to live life without a conscious connection to a loving source. Now, I have a new foundation for a life that works. With love all things are possible. The universe supports me in all things.

I understand that all things work for good when I come from love. Then I realize that the future will be better. Good results could come from my new mind-set and loving motivation. I just do the next indicated thing in front of me. What are the most loving things I can do for others, and myself? This becomes my new way of thinking.

The Law of Attraction

It is my vibrational offering that equals my point of attraction. Therefore, what you are thinking and doing is coming back to you as a vibrational match. The Universal Laws are *laws of love*. They attract love back to you. Cayce says, "All force in nature, all matter, is a form of vibration." He also says, "Everything is vibratory." Resolution is only available in a high-altered state of consciousness that is free of toxic elements and past emotional trauma. Therefore, it is necessary to use a means or method that allows your energy to flow into a higher emotional level of well-being most people call meditation or an altered state of being.

A popular Universal Law is the Law of Attraction. When you apply this information, you will attract to you an enriched life. With thoughts of being spiritually wealthy, healthy, and self-less, you will attract wealth, health, and opportunities to be of service to those around you. "But, seek ye first the kingdom of God, and his righteousness; and all these things shall be added unto you." My spiritual quality, not quantity, creates the higher level of my vibrations to ascend into unconditional love and maturity.

Knowing that I came to change my energy into compassion, forgiveness, gratitude, and unconditional love, solves the mystery of why I am here. Altering and transforming my vibrations back to those of the Creator's love attracts me to return to my spiritual home. This is the great inner urging of my soul to become complete. Healing the soul is my reason for being here.

My needs are met through a truthful focus with an open heart. My supply occurs. "God's grace is sufficient." When I merge my energy with that of the source of my being, abundance, health, and love, which is my inheritance, will manifest. I am being in the flow of a loving spiritual energy. I feel the bliss and prosperity.

What is Prayer and Meditation?

Prayer and Meditation raise me into an altered state of consciousness, where the ego cannot dominate my thinking and the solution to my problem can be a rational, loving one. Real prayer is going within and experiencing the merging of your spirit with God. In the process, I align and merge my love to the spirit of the universe. I become "One with the Source'."

Prayer and meditation are the direct way to connect with my Higher Power. My actions and thinking are now coming from a loving motivation. In a higher consciousness, the spiritual energy provides my needs.

In the book, *The Little Prince* by Antoine de Saint-Exupéry, it says, "Here is my secret. It's quite simple: One sees clearly only with the heart. Anything essential is invisible to the eyes."

Meditating on a daily basis builds a firm foundation for emotional balance. Self-searching prayer and meditation is very practical. Correct understanding of prayer and meditation makes this transformation possible.

"Mind is the builder." Edgar Cayce also said that spirit was our source and the physical was our result. From his famous quote, we learn that our mind can merge with its source or spirit to create the good results, inspirations, or solutions in our lives.

Healing ourselves can occur during meditation, regression therapy/hypnosis for childhood issues, or in a past-life regression. Healing only occurs in a higher state of love. Prayer, meditation, and hypnosis are ways to move into an altered state of consciousness where this change can occur. This change is most meaningful when done in an altered state, when you are in your heart.

This simple way is always available to set free the barriers that are blocking off the sunlight of the spirit from your life, allowing the grace of God to increase and grow. Releasing the obstacles or my negative emotions, and replacing them with love and grace, allows my spark of divinity in my heart to manifest and expand. Your spark of divinity is in your heart, it needs space to expand. God is energy in expansion.

One day, while in meditation after reading a Biblical

passage in Psalms, I got the message: *You were born happy, confident, and assertive. You are a good person. I made you that way.* I decided to give up the old messages from my family. Through meditation, I found an elevated level of myself and that I was already perfect in the eyes of the universe as I was created in the image of God.

Only experience transforms your energy into a healthy and happy life. Techniques like Therapeutic Hypnosis, which is a guided meditation, can provide a safe experience to move beyond the past into living in the "Now." It opens the door to the love in your life that can now motivate your life. Today a connection through meditation brings an inner guidance from my Higher Power. This spiritual conscious contact is the most important part of my life.

Meditation answered my concerns about having Bipolar Disorder. "Do you want to walk out of your Bipolar Disorder as your mother could not walk out of her prison of fear called Paranoid-Schizophrenia?" I responded after a moment of thought about what this meant. "Yes," I replied. The silent voice inside surprised me as I was not expecting to hear anything.

As I applied the tools in this chapter, I found myself not overreacting in my behavior as extremely. Gradually, when I was off all medications, I was able to see when I went back to old conduct. Several years later, with new healthy behaviors and thinking, my psychiatrist declared I was sane. I can have minor relapses, but I am aware quickly today, and know that acting rationally instead of reacting will restore my sanity.

I returned from Europe, visiting the sights where Mother Mary appeared. After going through the Baths at Lourdes, I went into a big episode of PTSD. All the loving energy for healing at the baths released the submerged feelings of many traumatic experiences. I was overwhelmed in anxiety. Through this difficult time, I had to give up my radio show that I produced and hosted. In meditation, Archangel Michael told me to go for additional therapy to remove consciously the very deep rage and anger within me from my childhood and adult abuse, that could now surface and leave. After releasing an unfathomable hidden rage, my peace and serenity began to emerge.

Again, meditation brought me awareness. I became fearless when I decided after many requests from a friend to ride a huge Ferris wheel on the waterfront of Seattle. I had a panic attack on the octopus when I was growing up that caused me to never ride any similar ride again, especially if it went up far above the ground.

In meditation, I came to the understanding that I could replace my fear with faith. I visualized my heavenly father holding me in his arms throughout the time of my ride. I would be safe in his embrace. For me meditation is practical, sagacious, and produces sanity. My reward for facing my last fear was a beautiful orange sunset as my Ferris wheel ride was at the top of the wheel. An orange sky appeared representing fearlessness, maturity, or Christ Consciousness.

Through appropriate subconscious healing and meditation for the root of the distress or illness, negative energy comes into awareness to leave. There is a better way than prescriptions to heal any sickness and/or emotional circumstances. However, without a therapist who has achieved this recovery, the results are nil because there is no supportive energy connection. Therapeutic Hypnosis is a kinder and more effective approach than typical therapy, because achieving emotional and spiritual harmony heals the soul; there are no longer symptoms to medicate. Damaged souls can transform into wholeness, health, and happiness.

When you understand this principle, it becomes easy to differentiate between what raises your vibrations closer to your Creator and what keeps you at a distance. People raise their energy by also using tuning forks, receiving laying-on-of-hands, and positive intentions. Other means include taking homeopathic remedies, herbs, drinking pure water, and eating non-toxic foods. Dr Gerber also adds, "The point is that we must begin to investigate alternative healing methods for what they can teach us about ourselves as evolving spiritual beings, as well as for their treatments of ailments for which orthodox medicine can do very little."

Surprising results from meditation occurred. Through my 31 years of spiritual growth and meditating daily, my life transformed in numerous ways. While practicing meditation, I first began to hear the silent still voice inside, and then I gradually became aware of being psychic. As I practiced this new skill and continued deeper and longer meditations, I found that I was a medium talking to and for ascended masters, including Jesus, Mother Mary, God, Masters, and Archangels. I regularly hold live channelings. I also can channel those passed over for their loved ones.

Love and Service

Prayer and meditation tune you into a higher power, just like tuning a radio. Think of your mind as a radio that needs to adjust to the correct station for guidance and help. Prayer and meditation raise you to a higher vibrational signal, allowing for proper attunement. "Prayer in action is love; love in action is service," said Mother Theresa. Your eyes now see the Christ in each heart around you. "Through the eyes of God" now means you are in service to those around you.

Now, I feel like my needs are met, and I am ready to pass on support, caring, and helping others when and where it is helpful. Ultimately, I found my life blossoms when I contribute to others. Service brings great energy for healing to the universe.

Probably the most famous person in service was Mother Teresa. We cannot all do the same kind of service she did; however, I can find a way to take a neighbor without a car to the grocery store. I can send a few dollars to help the needy. I can give a smile to those I walk by each day. There are so many ways to do this. Try volunteering, helping those less fortunate, or visiting a friend in a nursing home.

The Museum of Flight in Seattle, Washington, is totally dependent on volunteers. This amazing museum is manned with people who are trained to give tours, talks and answer questions to the thousands of international visitors. How often are you out there contributing to your community or organizations?

Finding Freedom

To open my mind to new perceptions is to stop blindly following old ideas and think for myself. To educate myself to new ways of being is to create a healthier and happier life. When I live in the present, I am in reality and the laws of the universe can facilitate my growth, when I apply them.

Moving into the higher energy of loving vibration offers a higher quality of life. Moreover, it feels wonderful. When this occurs, you are living beyond the third dimension of duality with good, bad and judgment. You have moved into a higher dimension of unconditional love and maturity. No longer a victim, you feel good. This is co-creating while totally enjoying life's experiences and having fun.

Today, my life has grown into healing all parts of my life, including the physical and medical issues in addition to the mental and emotional parts of my being. My inner self has released the blockages and obstacles of the third dimension through meditation and other supportive tools, to grow out of the mind-set of third dimension's duality. "For he, or she, that is without fear is free indeed," said Edgar Cayce. What a feeling! Love is!

Bliss

By Marilyn Redmond

Daily practice with tools of change
reveals freedom from fears, guilt, shame.
Releasing deep emotions through prayers, meditation
allows space for grace, love.
Self-respect blooms in the sunlight of spirit.
Bliss arrives to fill my soul
and tells me I am whole.

© 2010

Epilogue

I have learned so much in my many years. The most important information I want to share with you. What a surprise to find that everything I experience, I scripted before I came to Earth. Every experience I had was necessary and were the energies I needed to change to align with the loving creative forces of the universe.

I wish I had learned at the beginning to embrace all of life because they are my lessons; they are not good or bad. I found that the people and situations in my life are playing their part to help me move into a higher consciousness. Some people in my life had difficult roles to play.

Accepting the fact that when I react in fear, I am in an illusion instead of seeing truth was novel. In addition, I learned that resentments are unrealistic expectations of an angry child who did not get their way. When I release my fears and angers, it allows me to mature and move into reality.

Understanding that what I resist persists became significant. Resistance creates my difficulties and pain. It cuts me off from the sunlight of spirit. If I run from my problems, they return as larger ones or another medical problem to resolve emotionally. They return in another sickness or predicament. If I look outside myself for answers, my pain or troubles do not leave. No one can save me or heal me. Finding out that pain becomes illness after a time and is a symptom of a deeper problem was intriguing. It is an inside job.

In addition, I learned that if I am in the "Now," the past has no influence over me. Therefore, learning to live one moment at a time and enjoy the adventure opens the door to reality. In this new state of mind, I found my function is to be an instrument through which the presence of God can touch humanity. Living in reality is the supreme success on Earth. Enjoy the light!

Blessings, Marilyn

Rev. Marilyn L. Redmond
BA, CHT, IBRT

Marilyn is a minister for spiritual counseling, readings, tarot, regression/past life therapy, and channeling masters, archangels, Jesus and more. She is able to bring in your loved ones through her channeling. Reverend Marilyn Redmond has a degree in education. She is an International Speaker, International award-winning Writer, International Author, International Counselor and Consultant, International Columnist for *The Sussex Newspaper,* and an artist.

Her understanding and wisdom of the human dilemma and the solutions come from her experience and her spiritual guides. It will work for you, too. She is internationally board certified to do regression, and past life therapy (IBRT). She is a member of the American Board of Hypnotherapy (ABH). She was in *Who's Who for Professionals and Executives* for her pioneering and innovative work in restoring traumatic lives, healing emotional causes of illness and releasing negative energy.

She is also an extraordinary artist, reported *Vibrations,* newspaper of the American Institute of Holistic Theology. In addition, Marilyn sees your angels and paints their portraits or your family and animal portraits by commission.

Her recent book, *Paradigm Busters, Reveal the Real You*, is the ultimate "how to" book for achieving enlightenment and ascension. Marilyn is included in many anthologies. The latest anthologies are *Success Uncovered,* which has her chapter about achieving a spiritual life. In *The Book of Success,* she writes about applying spiritual principles in business and a career. *Walking Your Life* is the story of her ascension.

Her previous book, *The Real Meaning of 2012, A New Paradigm Bringing Heaven to Earth*, describes reducing the ego. Marilyn's first book, *Roses Have Thorns, Encouragement on evolving from pain to joy,* chronicles her traumatic life that ultimately brought the realization to transform her life.

Her eight books include her eBooks that are available at *http://www.amazon.com/MarilynRedmond/e/B0069WIKDC.* Her blog is *http://marilynredmondbooks.blogspot.com.*

Her many lectures, interviews, and "Channeling from Higher Realms" appear on You Tube.

https://www.youtube.com/results?search_query= marilyn+redmond&page=1

Her newsletter is http://eepurl.com/73fEH

Her web site is ***angelicasgifts.com*** for her countless articles, columns, radio shows, art, and TV appearance.

She is available for speaking, interviews, seminars, individual counseling, and readings.

Contact her at *marilyn@angelicasgifts.com* or 253-845-4907.

Publications by Marilyn L. Redmond

Books

Paradigm Busters, Reveal the Real You, Mithra Publishing, © 2016
The Real Meaning of 2012, A New Paradigm for Bringing Heaven to Earth, Dreamtime Press, © 2014
Roses Have Thorns; Encouragement on Evolving from Pain to Joy — Poetry, Kaleidoscope Press, © 1999

E-Books on Amazon.com

Vasanas, The Gifts That Show Us the Way
Incest, Love Heals the Soul
All Time Victim, Domestic Violence
Spiritual Alignment, Are You Ready for 2012
Peace on Earth, Finding Your New Life

Anthologies — Prose

The Book of Success, "New Glasses Bring Success," © 2016
    http://mithrapublishing.com/product/the-book-of-success
Hidden Success, "Beyond the Barriers to Success," © 2016
    http://mithrapublishing.com
Walking Your Life, "I Wanted to Live," © 2016
    http://mithrapublishing.com
Creating Your Life: Mindfulness and Meditation, "Love Never Fails," © 2016
    athenapublishing.com
Grand-Stories, Ernie Wendell, Friendly Oaks Publications, pp. 60-61
    © 2000
Recovery, "Pygmalion," an anthology, John M. Daniel, Editor,
    © 1994.

Published Poetry Single and Anthologies

- "Peace At Last," Poetry.com © 2012
    http://poetry.com/poems/149784?selected=reviews#comments
- "My-Gala-Celebration," http://poetry.com/poems/145132
- "Harmony," http://poetry.com/poems/86120
- "The-Light-of-Truth," http://poetry.com/poems/85867
- "VISION-A NEW ME," *Spiritually Speaking*, © 2006
- "Love," *First Word Bulletin*, Spain © 1997
- "Parade of Dreams," *First Word Bulletin*, Spain, © 1997.

- "Forever Christmas," *First Word Bulletin*, Spain © 1995
- "Pretty Baby-II," *When We Were Young: Childhood*, A Community of Voices, poem, © 2000
- *When We Were Young: Adulthood*, A Community of Voices, art, © 2000
- *Hot Dog, A Community of Voices*, art, Santa Barbara Writers, © 1999
- "Nearly Perfect," *Winging It With Words*, A Community of Voices, and art, Santa Barbara Writers, © 1997
- "Pretty Baby-I," *Poetry*—The Twenty-fourth Annual SFWC, © 1996
- "Leaving Home," *Silence Captured Still,* Tacoma Writers Club, © 1994
- "Love," *Our World's Most Treasured Poems*, World of Poetry Press, © 1991